Going Under

Discussions on

Baptism

Going Under

Discussions on

Baptism

Jim Elliff

Christian Communicators Worldwide

Additional copies of *Going Under—Discussions on Baptism* and other publications may be ordered online at *www.CCWonline.org*.

Going Under—Discussions on Baptism is published by
Christian Communicators Worldwide
Kansas City (Parkville), Missouri, USA.

Cover design by Thomas Jones

www.CCWonline.org

Table of Contents

I should think it a high sin and treason against heaven,
if, believing that baptism signifieth immersion,
and immersion only, I should pretend to administer it
by sprinkling; or, believing that baptism appertaineth
to believers only, I should consider myself a criminal
in the sight of God if I should give it to any but
those who believe.

As long as you give baptism to an unregenerate child,
people will imagine that it must do the child good;
for they will ask, if it does not do it any good,
why is it baptized?

~ C. H. Spurgeon

Introduction

We should never take baptism lightly. From the inception of the church to our present day, many have suffered and even died for it.

Though baptism does not in itself save, it does shout out our identity with Christ. When that public declaration is made, many pay a huge price. It is not just a meaningless ritual, or merely a duty; it is a privilege of the highest sort.

Some who are reading this are preparing for baptism now. You are doing the right thing. This book will add some meaning to your experience. Others are confused. Perhaps you were sprinkled as an infant and wonder whether something more should be done. Still others of you are concerned believers who want to be as informed as possible so that you can help others.

Baptism is a command from Christ Himself. Here is some biblical help in understanding it better.

Jim Elliff
Kansas City, Missouri
www.CCWonline.org

Discussion One:
Believers or Babies?

Are you a Christian? That is, have you come to Christ on His terms of repentance and faith? If so, let me ask you a question: If God makes it clear to you through the Bible that you need to be baptized, would you be happy to obey Him?

Yes, of course.

Good! Because any person who understands God's will, yet would *not* be willing to obey Him, is likely not a true Christian. I know that sounds a little strong, but it is what the Bible says (cf. John 14:15; 1 John 2:3-4).

That's OK. I don't need to be baptized anyway, because I've already been baptized—as a baby!

I see, but are you sure you were baptized? Is water sprinkled on a baby (called *aspersion*) or poured on the head of a baby (called *infusion*) really what Jesus intended? Maybe in a warm and meaningful way, you just got wet. Of course, I don't mean to be rude. It's OK for babies to get wet, but the Bible never calls this baptism.

Then, at what age should we be baptized? As children?

Maybe.

As teens?

Maybe.

As adults?

Maybe.

As babies?

In my view, never.

But you are asking the wrong question. A better question is this: *Who* is to be baptized? And the answer to that is, *believers*—children who are believers (if we can be reasonably certain they *are* believers), teen believers, and adult believers. But *never* infant believers, because there is no such thing. As far as we know, infants are *unable* to understand and believe. Even if they could, they would be unable to express their faith in ways that would give us reason to baptize them.

But Jesus baptized babies! After all, He said, "Let the little children come to Me, and do not forbid them; for of such is the kingdom of heaven."

Stop and think. Jesus did say that (cf. Matthew 19:13-15; Mark 10:13-16), but there is no reason to believe He was referring to baptism. No reputable Bible translation even hints that Jesus baptized the children who were brought to Him. In fact, we are plainly told what He *did* do: He took them in His arms, laid His hands on them, and blessed them. Jesus never baptized a baby and He never told us to baptize a baby—*ever*.

The passage does teach us to encourage children to come to Christ in prayer, learning from His Word, seeking to know Him, but a child can never be converted until he or she has true faith in Christ—just like an adult. *Any* person who comes with such faith is part of the kingdom. That is why Jesus goes on to say, "Assuredly, I say to you, whoever does not receive the kingdom of God *as* [or *like*] a little child will by no means enter it" (emphasis mine). A child's willingness to trust an adult is an illustration of what every person must exhibit in coming to Christ—childlike trust in Him alone.

But surely Jesus baptized some babies.

No, never.

But the disciples must have.

Sorry, never. In John 4:1-2, the disciples "made and baptized" disciples (i.e., followers), but babies were not among them, because babies cannot be disciples.

In every case in the New Testament the answer is the same—only believers were baptized. Let's look at the passages:

- **3000 at Pentecost**—Acts 2:41
  "Then those who gladly received his word were baptized. . . ."

- **Samaritan converts**—Acts 8:12
  "But when they believed Philip as he preached the things concerning the kingdom of God and the name of Jesus Christ, both men and women were baptized."

- **Simon the Sorcerer**—Acts 8:13
  "Then Simon himself also believed; and when he was baptized he continued with

11

Philip. . . ." (Simon proved to be a false
convert, but the order is the same.)

- **The eunuch**—Acts 8:36-39
  "Now as they went down the road, they
  came to some water. And the eunuch said,
  'See, here is water. What hinders me from
  being baptized?' Then Philip said, 'If you
  believe with all your heart, you may.' And
  he answered and said, 'I believe that Jesus
  Christ is the Son of God.' So he commanded the chariot to stand still. And both
  Philip and the eunuch went down into the
  water, and he baptized him. Now when
  they came up out of the water . . ." (I just
  included this last part to show you that he
  was immersed—but I'm getting ahead of
  myself. We'll save the question of "mode"
  for another lesson.)

- **Saul of Tarsus (Paul)**—Acts 9:18
  "Immediately there fell from his eyes something like scales, and he received his sight
  at once; and he arose and was baptized." (Note: Paul was baptized *after* his
  Damascus Road salvation experience).

- **The household of Cornelius**—Acts
  10:47-48
  "'Can anyone forbid water, that these
  should not be baptized who have received
  the Holy Spirit just as we have?' And he
  commanded them to be baptized in the
  name of the Lord. . . ."

- **The household of Lydia**—Acts 16:14-15
  "The Lord opened her heart to heed the
  things spoken by Paul. And when she and
  her household had been baptized . . ."

- **The household of the Philippian jailer—** Acts 16:31-34
  "So they said, 'Believe on the Lord Jesus Christ, and you will be saved, you and your household.' Then they spoke the word of the Lord to him and to all who were in his house. And he took them the same hour of the night and washed their stripes. And immediately he and all his family were baptized. Now when he had brought them into his house, he set food before them; and he rejoiced, having believed in God with all his household."

- **The household of Crispus and other Corinthians—**Acts 18:8
  "Then Crispus, the ruler of the synagogue, believed on the Lord with all his household. And many of the Corinthians, hearing, believed and were baptized."

So, there you have it. As far as the Bible is concerned there is not one place where a baby is baptized. Only believers are baptized. But here is something else to consider . . .

Not only is every example of baptism in the New Testament that of believers rather than babies, but Christ Himself *commands* the church to baptize believers. Remember, the church is built upon Christ as the chief cornerstone, with the foundation of the New Testament apostles and prophets (Ephesians 2:20; 3:5). Here then is Christ's command to these apostles who were to teach the rest of us: "Go therefore and make disciples of all the nations, baptizing *them* in the name of the Father and of the Son and of the Holy Spirit, teaching *them* to observe all things that I have commanded you; and lo, I am with you always, even to the end of the age" (Matthew 28:19-20, emphasis mine).

This means that the church is under obligation to baptize *disciples*. If they baptize babies, who cannot be disciples (nor can they be taught all that Christ commands), then they are doing something other than what Christ specifically commanded. He is the final word on this, for He is the one who said, "All authority has been given to Me in heaven and on earth" (v. 18).

By the way, this is why this act of obedience is called an "ordinance." It has been ordered by Christ Himself.

But the Matthew 28 passage doesn't tell us not to baptize babies.

True, but that isn't a very sound argument. The point is, we are told to make disciples and to baptize *them* and teach *them*. Any plain reading of this text leaves us no other persons to baptize. These are some of Christ's last words on earth, given in the form of a charge or a commission. The passage is too encompassing, directional, and well-illustrated in the New Testament to admit of exceptions or additions. If we could make exceptions or add another form of practice to this, then why not put in anything we want? For instance, why not baptize our pets? Jesus never told us *not* to do that either.

In the absence of any illustration of baby baptism in the New Testament, we are hard-pressed to think that the disciples understood Jesus to allow for baby baptism by not forbidding it in the Great Commission.

But my baptism as an infant meant a great deal to my parents.

I'm sure that is true, but our emotions are not Christ. As Christians we follow Christ. Enjoy emotions, but don't obey them.

But so many people can't be wrong!

They can, because either *we* are wrong or *they* are—
and each group is "so many people." But, I cannot
question anyone's sincerity, and I do believe that sometimes true Christians differ on this issue. There are
theological reasons why some people baptize babies.
There are also "tradition" reasons. But when all is said
and done, we must admit that Christ never commanded
baby baptism, nor practiced it, nor did his followers
teach or practice it. And that ought to send a message.

The baptism of babies cannot be found *explicitly* anywhere in the Bible. The best that anyone says (even its
strongest advocates) is that it is *implied.* But the Bible
speaks plainly and sufficiently about our essential ac-
tions, especially in such a basic issue as baptism. It is a
big stretch to build such a practice out of uncertain im-
plications where there is neither instruction nor example to affirm it.

If Christ ordered baptism for *believers*, and you are a
true believer, then will you happily do what Christ
commands? Surely Christ has it right. And whatever is
right is . . . well . . . right for you.

Discussion Two:
Sprinkle or Immerse?

I heard that George Whitefield, the prominent English preacher during the Great Awakening of the 1740s, once said, "All my chickens have become ducks." Why did he say that?

Because so many of his converts, who had originally been sprinkled as babies, were now being baptized by immersion.

Why would they do that?

Because many of those who had been converted as adults during the Awakening had discovered that the biblical mode of baptism is immersion *following belief in Christ*. This means that they no longer considered what happened to them as infants real baptism.

Deciding between infant baptism and believer's baptism has been a longstanding issue. The early churches practiced immersion, as we will see. Eighteenth-century German Lutheran minister and church historian Johann Lorenz von Mosheim said, "In this century [referring to the 1st century], baptism was administered in convenient places, without [outside] the public assemblies, and by immersing the candidates wholly in water."

The Eastern [Greek] Orthodox Church has always practiced immersion. And if anyone would be expected to understand the *Greek* word for baptism found in the New Testament, it would be the *Greek* Orthodox theologians.

Even Catholics practiced immersion until the 14th century, except in unusual cases. Consider this quote from the *Edinburgh Encyclopedia*:

> It is impossible to mark the precise period when sprinkling was introduced. It is probable, however, that it was invented in Africa, in the second century, in favor of clinics [i.e., when the person was too ill to be immersed]. But it was so far from being approved by the church in general that the Africans themselves did not account it valid.

> The first law for sprinkling was obtained in the following manner: Pope Stephen III, being driven from Rome by Astulphus, king of the Lombards, in 753, fled to Papin, who, a short time before, had usurped the crown of France. While he remained there, the monks of Cressy, in Brittany, consulted him whether, in a case of necessity, baptism performed by pouring water on the head of the infant would be lawful. Stephen replied that it would. But, though the truth of this fact should be allowed, which some Catholics deny, yet pouring or sprinkling was only admitted in cases of necessity.

> It was not till 1311 that the legislature, in a council held at Revenna, declared immersion or sprinkling to be indifferent [that is, permissible either way]. In this country (Scotland), however, sprinkling was never practiced, in ordinary cases, until after the Reformation; and in England, even in the reign of Edward VI, trine

immersion—dipping first the right side, secondly the left side, and last the face of the infant—was commonly observed." –Art. *Baptism*

Interestingly, some of the 16th-century Reformers, men who we appreciate for parting with the Roman Catholic church on important issues of biblical doctrine, retained the practice of infant baptism and persecuted other Reformers who insisted on baptizing believers only by immersion (Anabaptists).

> In January, 1527, Felix Manz was drowned in the River Limmat for practicing believer's baptism. Zwingli's comment was, "Let him who talks about going under [the water] go under!" Ulrich Zwingli, the leader of the Reformation movement in Zurich, became a stormy upholder of infant baptism. However, look what Zwingli said: "Nothing grieves me more than at present I must baptize children, for I know it ought not to be done . . . but if I were to stop the practice of Infant Baptism, I would lose my office." And again, "I leave baptism [by immersion] untouched. I call it neither right nor wrong. If we were to baptize as Christ instituted it, then we would not baptize any person until he reached the years of discretion, for I find Infant Baptism nowhere written or practiced. But we must practice it now so as not to offend our fellow men. . . . It is better not to preach [believer's] baptism until the world is ready to receive it."(Brian Russell, *Baptism, Sign and Seal of God's Grace,* p. 26-27)

Later, Zwingli played a major role in constructing the theological system known as *Covenantalism* (see Discussion 4, pp. 33-39), which, for some groups, undergirds the practice of infant baptism.

Immersion versus sprinkling was also an issue with the framers of the famous Westminster Confession, the basic document of the Presbyterians (1644). In fact, the mode of sprinkling was granted by a majority of only one vote (25 vs. 24). Through the influence of Dr. Lightfoot the group was persuaded of the dangers of taking the immersion view. One fear was that many might leave the Presbyterians and become Baptists! (Lumpkin, *History of Immersion*, p. 35).

More chickens would become ducks!

But why is it so important to immerse instead of sprinkle?

For three reasons:

First, we immerse because that is the meaning of the word "baptize" in the original language (*baptizo*). The lexicons are consistent in stating this.

The normal words for sprinkling (*rantizo*) or pouring (*ekcheo*) were not used for baptism in the Bible though used often elsewhere. In fact, even John Calvin, a paedobaptist (one who baptizes babies, usually by sprinkling), believed that "immersion" was the meaning of the word. He said,

> Whether the person . . . be wholly immersed, and whether thrice or once, or whether water be only poured or sprinkled upon him, is of no importance; Churches ought to be left at liberty, in this respect, to act according to the difference of countries. The very word *baptize*, however, signifies to immerse; and it is certain that immersion was the practice of the ancient Church. (Allen translation of Calvin's *Institutes*, p. 599)

Presbyterian theologian Robert Rayburn says, "No scholar of any stature argues that the primary meaning of this word is not *to dip*" (Robert Rayburn, *What About Baptism?* Baker, p. 25).

There are many who practice sprinkling or pouring who admit to the original meaning of this word. (See Appendix 2, *Historical Quotes Concerning the Mode and Subjects of Baptism.*)

Secondly, immersion is clearly what happened. Note what the Scripture shows us:

Water was used.

Acts 10:47-48: "'Can anyone forbid water that these should not be baptized who have received the Holy Spirit just as we have?' And he commanded them to be baptized in the name of the Lord."

Much water was necessary.

John 3:23 reads as follows: "Now John also was baptizing in Aenon near Salim, because there was much water there. And they came and were baptized."

Why did the Spirit include the words, "because there was much water there" if sprinkling were John's practice? If he sprinkled, he could do that with a cup of water anywhere he wanted. John Calvin clearly recognized the significance of these words when he wrote, "From these words, we may infer that John and Christ administered baptism by plunging the whole body beneath the water" (*Commentaries*, Vol. 17, p. 130).

People came to the water.

Acts 8:36 says: "Now as they went down the road, they came to some water. And the eunuch said, 'See, here is water. What hinders me from being baptized?'"

Again, the eunuch traveling across the desert surely had water in his chariot, but it is only when they "came to some water" that he thought it possible to be baptized.

People went down into the water.

Acts 8:38 states: "So he commanded the chariot to stand still. And both Phillip and the eunuch went down into the water, and he baptized him."

You do not need to go "down into the water" to sprinkle somebody. No, going "down into the water" implies immersion. Once again John Calvin recognized the obvious meaning of these words, writing, "Here we see the rite used among men of old time in baptism; for they put all the body into the water" (*Commentaries*, Vol. 18, p. 364).

People came up out of the water.

Mark 1:9-10 states: "It came to pass in those days that Jesus came from Nazareth of Galilee, and was baptized by John in the Jordan. And immediately, coming up from the water, He saw the heavens parting and the Spirit descending upon Him like a dove."

Acts 8:39 also says, "they came up out of the water." They came *up out of* the water, because they had gone *down into* the water to be immersed.

You're right. That seems clear. What is the third reason?

Third, immersion is the correct picture of what has happened to the believer spiritually. We will look at this issue in our next discussion.

Isn't it true that Mark 7:4 shows that "baptizo" could be defined as something other than "to dip or immerse"? It is used twice in that verse, first for the Pharisees' ceremonial "washing" of themselves, and then for the washing of cups, pitchers, and copper pots. Some translations even include the washing of couches. Certainly they did not fully immerse themselves and all of these other items.

First of all, noted Greek scholar W. Robertson Nicole says of the first use of *baptizo* in this verse (the Pharisees' washing before eating) that it "may be interpreted either as dipping of the *hands* . . . or bathing of the *whole body*" (quoted from *The Expositor's Greek Testament*, Vol. 1, Eerdman's, p. 387). Either way, he defines it as "to dip or immerse."

And if complete immersion of the body, or the ceremonial immersion of other physical objects seems too odd to be true, consider the fact that many Jewish homes had a *miqveh*, or ceremonial bath. A prominent Jewish authority says, "In all cases of ritual impurity it was necessary for the person or object to be immersed in a bath built in accordance with the rules laid down by the Rabbis" (*The Jewish Encyclopedia*, NY: KTAV Publishing, p. 588). It had to be able to hold 87 U.S. gallons. Another way of measuring it would add up to 151 U.S. gallons. It must be "sufficient water to cover entirely the body of a man of average size" (p. 588). So, coming from the marketplace, a strict Pharisee might indeed immerse himself in order to be ceremonially clean. Jesus was making fun of such strict Pharisees who would not come in from the marketplace without immersing themselves completely in water!

Wouldn't it be impossible to immerse 3000 people in one day, as on the Day of Pentecost (Acts 2)?

Not at all. For one thing, there were perhaps more people who administered baptism than just the apostles. Perhaps the 70 who were sent out by Christ earlier were involved, or maybe others. Also, there was a lot of water there. Murray Adamthwaite writes:

> So far 48 *miqveh* pools have been discovered in connection with the temple mount dating to Herod's Temple. . . . Added to this were the various pools and cisterns either under the Temple platform or on its perimeter, 34 in all. . . . Then there were the pools in the Jerusalem area, e.g. the Pool of Bethesda . . . the pool of Hezekiah and the Serpent's Pool. (Murray Adamthwaite, "Baptism Is Immersion" (*Reformation Today* #109, p. 34)

It certainly *could have* been accomplished.

In fact, it *was*.

Discussion Three:
Symbolize or Save?

We said there were three reasons why we immerse people instead of sprinkling them.

First, "immersion" is the meaning of the word *baptizo*.

Christ and his apostles consistently used the word, *baptizo*, not the Greek words for "sprinkle" or "pour," to tell us what to do. It is the same word (or its derivative) that is used for the rich man's request in Hades when he asked for Lazarus to "dip" his finger in water and touch his tongue. It is the word used when Jesus "dipped" his bread during the last supper, and it was used in the Septuagint (Greek translation of the Old Testament) concerning the man who "dipped" seven times in the Jordan. The word consistently means "to dip or immerse." It is incomprehensible that God would have made so basic and universal a command confusing to his disciples (cf. Matthew 28:19-20).

The second reason we immerse is because that is precisely what happened in the New Testament. The passages indicate that baptism took place where there were bodies of water. The people came to the water, went down into the water, and came up out of the water.

The third reason we immerse is because immersion best pictures what God means to show through the ordinance.

And what is that?

The main purpose of baptism is to symbolize or drama-
tize *physically* what has already happened to the believer *spiritually*. At his conversion (not at baptism) the
believer was brought into union with Christ in His
death, burial, and resurrection (Romans 6:3-8; Colossians 2:12) *and* he was cleansed or washed spiritually
(1 Corinthians 6:11; Titus 3:5). Both of these *spiritual*
aspects of conversion are best depicted by the *physical*
act of immersion in water. We commonly refer to it as
an outward sign of an inward reality.

Why do you say, "symbolize" rather than "save"?

Because water baptism is an outward act with physical
elements (our bodies and water) that, in themselves,
have no power to change us spiritually. Some groups
practice an immersion which to them is not symbolic.
For them, immersion in water either saves or is a necessary component in salvation. I think they are wrong.
They make baptism a work necessary for salvation, and
therefore corrupt the meaning of grace and faith (see
Ephesians 2:8-9).

And you don't?

That's right. I don't—because there are so many passages that make it clear that *believers* are the ones being baptized. God's grace has acted on behalf of these
people and they have been enabled therefore to exercise
saving faith in Christ—all *before* they are baptized in
water. They have true faith and grace first. You may
refer back to the list of Scriptures in our first discussion
that affirm this (pp. 11-13).

But aren't there some verses that say baptism saves you? Surely these people do this because they think they have God's view of it?

Right, I think they are generally sincere. But their error is a critical one. I have written out some helps for understanding these few passages in Appendix 1.

Let me remind you of the clear case of the Gentiles who heard the gospel from Peter at Cornelius' house. As Peter spoke to these people, the Spirit fell on them just like had happened at Pentecost. The Christians that had come with Peter "were astonished . . . because the gift of the Holy Spirit had been poured out on the Gentiles also." It was *after* this acknowledgement that Peter asks, "'Can anyone forbid water that these should not be baptized who have received the Holy Spirit just as we have?' And he commanded them to be baptized" (Acts 10:47-48).

Note the following:

- The Holy Spirit was received prior to their being baptized. The Holy Spirit brings the life of Christ to the believer. Therefore, they were already alive by the Spirit before being baptized. John said, "By this we know that we abide in Him, and He in us, because He has given us of His Spirit" (1 John 4:13). John went on to say, "this is the testimony: that God has given us eternal life, and this life is in His Son. He who has the Son has life; he who does not have the Son of God does not have life" (1 John 5:11-12). To "have the Son" is the same as having the Spirit, of course, and therefore the same as having eternal life.

- The group that came along with Peter *knew* that these Gentiles had this life prior to their baptism.

- Peter states that these people had "believed" prior to their baptism.

- Peter had previously declared in his message to them that "whoever believes in Him will receive remission [forgiveness] of sins" (v. 43). Therefore the people in Cornelius' house were already forgiven people *before* they were baptized.

So, it was believing people who had the Spirit, whom Peter and the other Christians *knew* were already believers, that were baptized. If this is the case, then baptism cannot save or help to save, but must rather be symbolic of the change that has already occurred.

I've always wondered why the thief on the cross next to Jesus was allowed into Paradise without baptism.

It is certainly not enough to say, "Had he lived, he would have been baptized, therefore you must see him as though he were baptized." We all admit that he would have been baptized. I believe all Christians who know baptism to be a clear act of obedience would certainly obey the Lord, especially on this very first command following their conversion.

Some may argue that the thief was saved under an Old Testament dispensation and therefore did not need water baptism. But this is not so. Christ Himself said the Kingdom of God was near, and He went about having His disciples baptize converts *prior to* His death and resurrection.

Concerning this symbolism, I guess I don't understand the idea of a spiritual union with Christ's death and resurrection. What does that mean?

Romans 6:3-8 shows us this union with Christ's death, burial, and resurrection beautifully, though the purpose of the passage is not to teach about baptism, but rather our freedom from the ultimate control of sin.

> Or do you not know that as many of us as were baptized into Christ Jesus were baptized into His death? Therefore we were buried with Him through baptism into death, that just as Christ was raised from the dead by the glory of the Father, even so we also should walk in newness of life.
>
> For if we have been united together in the likeness of His death, certainly we also shall be in the likeness of His resurrection, knowing this, that our old man was crucified with Him, that the body of sin might be done away with, that we should no longer be slaves of sin. For he who has died has been freed from sin. Now if we died with Christ, we believe that we shall also live with Him. . . .

We see in this intriguing passage that believers are considered to be in union with Christ, experiencing in His death and resurrection their own death and resurrection. That is, in Christ we died to sin when He died and we were raised to life when He was raised. God sees us "in Him." In many ways this language is unique and different, but the end result can be easily understood. Our union with Christ means that we have died to sin's domination and have been raised to live a new life toward God.

Paul ties this to the word *baptism*: He says we "were baptized into His death," "buried with Him through baptism into death," etc. Does he mean that this all happens when we are baptized with water? No. He is saying that our being *spiritually* "immersed" into Christ's death and resurrection produces these results—our death to sin and our life in Christ. It is our *spiritual* union with Christ that causes these benefits to come. It is a spiritual work that water cannot accomplish. Our water baptism, however, beautifully pictures or dramatizes this for others to see.

How does it picture it?

Going down into water, we act out our death and burial. Coming up out of the water, we act out our being raised to a new life in Christ. Sprinkling or pouring does not portray this.

What about cleansing from sin?

Well, there are those who believe that washing or cleansing by Christ is best seen in sprinkling. Yet again, they forget how strict Jews "washed" themselves and their items by immersion if they had been defiled in some way. To quote Rabbi Maimonides:

> Whenever in the law, washing of the flesh or of the clothes is mentioned, it means nothing else than the dipping of the whole body in a laver; for if any man dips himself all over, except the tip of his little finger, he is still in his uncleanness." (Hilchot, Celim. C. i. Sect. ii)

This was typically done in a *miqveh*, or private pool. I spoke of this earlier. So, it is right for us to think of washing as "dipping" or "immersion." Immersion is the best way to picture both the union with Christ in death and resurrection and the washing of forgiveness that takes place when a person comes to Christ. Immersion *symbolizes* but does not *cause* either the union or the cleansing.

Are you trying to get me to be baptized?

Sure. If you are a true believer, I'm commanded to (Matthew 28:19-20). God wants you to go through this beautiful and meaningful symbolic act to show others—your family and friends, and the church—just how Christ has changed you and cleansed you. Baptism preaches without words!

To go over it again, baptism is to occur *following* true conversion, not *before*. The mode of baptism in the early church was immersion. There is amazing agreement on this issue, even among paedobaptist scholars. We immerse because 1) it is the meaning of the word *baptizo*, 2) it was what actually happened in the New Testament, and 3) it is the perfect corresponding symbol for the actual union we experience with Christ in his death, burial, and resurrection and our cleansing from sin.

Discussion Four:
Refashioned
or New?

We have discussed the issue of when a person should be baptized—*after* he or she becomes a believer in Christ. Babies are never baptized in the Bible.

The 19th-century pastor, Charles Spurgeon tells his story this way (remember that the Church of England and Congregationalists practice infant baptism):

> The Church of England Catechism has in it, as some of you may remember, this question, "What is required of persons to be baptized?" and the answer I was taught to give, and did give, was, "Repentance whereby they forsake sin, and faith whereby they steadfastly believe the promises of God made to them in that sacrament." I looked that answer up in the Bible, and I found it to be strictly correct as far as repentance and faith are concerned, and of course, when I afterwards became a Christian I also became a Baptist; and here I am, and it is due to the Church of England Catechism that I am a Baptist.
>
> Having been brought up among Congregationalists, I had never looked into the matter in my life. I had thought myself to have been baptized

as an infant; and so, when I was confronted with the question, "What is required of persons to be baptized?" and I found that repentance and faith were required, I said to myself, "Then I have not been baptized; that infant sprinkling of mine was a mistake; and [if it] please God that I ever have repentance and faith, I will be properly baptized." . . . It led me, however, as I believe, to follow the Scriptural teaching that repentance and faith are required before there can be any true baptism.

We have affirmed as well that the mode of baptism should be immersion rather than pouring or sprinkling. We have also clarified that baptism does not save or help to save a person. It is an outward symbol of an inward reality. Now let's look at a matter overlapping these issues—Covenantalism as it relates to children.

Now you are making things hard to understand! What does that word mean?

Well, many Covenantalists (but not baptistic ones), believe babies should be baptized to be part of the "covenant family" just like Old Testament Jewish boys were circumcised to be part of the "covenant family" of the Jews. In the Covenantal view, the baptism of infants takes the place of circumcision and confers covenant benefits. Of course, Covenantalism is about more than this, and many Covenantalists stop short of infant baptism, as I mentioned.

I thought we already answered this. At least, it seems that it has been well-proven that babies were never baptized in the Bible and sprinkling is not the mode. A person must be a believer before being baptized.

Right. We did answer much of the question. But because some of our Protestant paedobaptist friends practice infant baptism while still firmly believing that people need to be converted if they are to go to heaven (unlike Catholics), we need to deal with this case separately. We share a lot in common with all Protestant paedobaptists who are Bible-believing Christians, and therefore we want to be sure of our differences while loving them as part of the body of Christ.

Let me state this as clearly as possible. The Covenantal position on baptism (the historical Reformed position) is that babies are baptized (usually by sprinkling) *not* to make them Christians (like the Catholics believe), and *not* merely as a way of dedicating them to God (as many Methodists see infant baptism), but to include them in the Covenant family. Additionally, in the historical Reformed view, infant baptism is *not* seen as a guarantee that the child will be converted later.

So what's the difference? I mean, if the baby is not guaranteed salvation through this plan, what is the difference between the baptistic position and theirs? Don't you believe that children are introduced to special blessings just by being in a Christian family?

I do. Frankly, this is one of the difficulties they face. There does not seem to be any evidence that their children are converted at any better rate than ours. Remember as well that Esau and Judas were circumcised as a sign, and were solidly in the Old Covenant, yet they were not converted. There are many such examples.

How did Covenantalists arrive at this plan?

A study of Covenantalism as it relates to infant baptism can get quite complicated, but it boils down to this:

Since there was a rite of initiation in the Old Testament period, then that rite should be in some way continued in the New Testament period. If *babies* received this rite of initiation into the Old Covenant, then *babies* ought to be the recipients of the rite in the New Covenant. That's a simple way to look at it.

What does the Bible teach, in your view?

The Bible does not teach us to refashion the Old Testament rite of circumcision by replacing it with baptism and performing it on babies. Rather, it teaches that when we become new creatures in Christ, at regeneration (when God gives life to our dead souls), we are experiencing the very thing circumcision pictured in the Old Testament. Circumcision of the *skin* in the Old Testament is replaced by the circumcision of the *heart* in the New Testament, not by baptism. There is no compelling reason to make *baptism* of babies a substitute for *circumcision* of babies.

Read the following New Testament passages, which I believe affirm this view. Note in each one that circumcision of the heart is the new Covenant parallel to the circumcision of the skin in the Old Covenant:

> In Him you were also circumcised with the circumcision made without hands, by putting off the body of the sins of the flesh, by the circumcision of Christ. (Colossians 2:11)

> For we are the circumcision, who worship God in the Spirit, rejoice in Christ Jesus, and have no confidence in the flesh. . . . (Philippians 3:3)

> For in Christ Jesus neither circumcision nor uncircumcision avails anything, but a new creation. (Galatians 6:15)

> For he is not a Jew who is one outwardly, nor
> is circumcision that which is outward in the
> flesh; but he is a Jew who is one inwardly; and
> circumcision is that of the heart, in the Spirit,
> not in the letter. . . . (Romans 2:28-29)

The future counterpart of Old Covenant circumcision
was even prophesied by Ezekiel in the Old Testament:

> I will give you a new heart, and put a new spirit
> within you; I will take the heart of stone out of
> your flesh and give you a heart of flesh.
> (Ezekiel 36:26)

Babies have not experienced this circumcision of the
heart. If they do, later, when they can express and give
evidence of their faith, *then* and only then should they
be baptized indicating outwardly, personally, and con-
sciously their place in the New Covenant.

The covenant in the Old Testament with the Jews was
temporal and had to do with a nation. It included many
who were not regenerate. The New Covenant is only
for the regenerate people of God. Physical circumcision
as a sign of membership into the nation of Israel was
perfectly reasonable. You could circumcise unregenerate babies into *that* covenant. But those in the New
Covenant are *all* converted. God established the symbol
of water baptism *following* regeneration because only
those who are true Christians are in the New Covenant.

In the section in Hebrews 8 about the New Covenant,
we are given, for instance, the plank of the Covenant
that says, "None of them shall teach his neighbor, and
none his brother, saying, 'Know the Lord,' for all shall
know Me, from the least of them to the greatest of
them" (Hebrews 8:11). In the Old Covenant most did
not know Him. But in the New, all do. Baptism is the

visible symbol of a person's entrance into the New
Covenant. Unless we can be reasonably confident that a
particular person (however young or old) knows the
Lord, we should not treat him as a member of the New
Covenant. There is simply no way to have such confi-
dence regarding infants or very young children.

Are there other reasons to avoid a Covenantal posi-tion on baptism?

Yes. Perhaps one of most convincing has to do with the
meeting of the early church called "The Jerusalem
Council." You remember that this section of Acts deals
with leaders who came to the people of God and said,
"Unless you are circumcised according to the custom of
Moses, you cannot be saved" (Acts 15:1). The Bible
says that Paul and Barnabas had "no small dissension
and dispute with them." It was decided that Paul and
Barnabas would go up to the apostles and elders to discuss this problem.

As you follow their arguments you see men who care
deeply about the truth and do not wish to dilute or pol-
lute the gospel. But there is one obvious void in the discussion. Nowhere does anyone say what ought to be the
obvious thing to say if you are Covenantal regarding
baptism. Nobody says, "Men, it isn't about circumcision, whether we should or shouldn't, because baptism
of babies has totally replaced circumcision as the symbol of entrance into the covenant!"

This same thing happens in the book of Galatians
where the idea of circumcision is talked about. Paul
never says, "Baptism of babies makes this a moot
point." Rather, he rules it out on other grounds. Christian circumcision is a circumcision of the heart.

But what about the place in the Bible where it says that children are holy if their parents are Christians?

You are referring to 1 Corinthians 7:14. First of all, that passage is not related to baptism at all. Secondly, if it does affirm the practice of baptizing unbelieving *children*, then it also affirms the baptism of the unbelieving *spouse* who is said to be "sanctified" through the believing spouse. But no one I know of uses this verse to justify baptizing unbelieving spouses.

This section was difficult, but I think I get it. One last question: What if I was sprinkled as an infant? Do I need to be baptized again since becoming a true Christian?

Well, we shouldn't call what happened to you "baptism." That's impossible to do with infants since they are not believers. So if you were to be baptized *now*, you would not be getting baptized *again*. It would be your *first* and *only* true baptism. But yes, if you have become a believer, you should be properly baptized *as a believer*. And this is a real joy and privilege!

Let me say this more emphatically. YES! Anyone who is a believer who has not been properly baptized, should do so—with joy!

Discussion Five:
Just Anyone or a True Church?

May I be baptized by just anyone?

No. Believers should be baptized by other believers who are acting within the structure of a local church. True local churches have been given the authority and responsibility to oversee essential Christian activities such as baptism.

With so many religious groups out there, what is a true local church?

The English word "church," in its broad contemporary sense, denotes a religious assembly that identifies with Christ, whether its beliefs are genuinely Christian or not (i.e., Baptist church, Methodist church, Catholic church, Mormon church, etc.). The Greek word from which we get "church" (*ecclesia*) is also used in the Bible in a broader sense, describing organized gatherings of Christians as well as, in at least one case, a local civic assembly (cf. Acts 19:39).

The only meaning of "church" I intend to convey here is that which I believe was intended by the Apostle Paul when he addressed various groups of Christians as "the church of God which is at Corinth" (1 Corinthians 1:2), "the churches of Galatia" (Galatians 1:2), "the church that is in their house" (Romans 16:5), etc. The differences between these uses of the word "church" (or *ecclesia*) and all other uses (whether in the Bible or in common usage) are not to be determined by a dictionary or lexicon. The differences are seen in what the *purpose* of these groups was, what they *believed*, and what they *practiced*. My own definition of a true local church *in that restricted sense* would be this:

> A church is a body of baptized believers gathering regularly to share life with Christ and each other, to affirm and proclaim His gospel, and to submit to His headship in doctrine and practice, according to His written Word.

Is every part of that definition essential?

Yes. If any aspect is completely missing, you do not have a true local church.

Think of a baseball team. Baseball, by definition, involves three activities: 1) throwing the ball, 2) catching the ball, and 3) hitting the ball with a bat. If nine skilled athletes get together to throw the ball and catch the ball, but construct a game in which they do not use a bat to hit the ball (or use a tennis racquet instead), they may not rightly be considered a baseball team. They may *call* themselves a baseball team. They may *dress* like baseball players. They may *gather on a baseball field*. But since they are neglecting, rejecting, or redefining one of the essential elements of the game, they are not playing baseball. And if they never play baseball, they are not a baseball team.

Lots of religious groups would say they believe and do the things that make them a church.

That's right. Let's look more closely at our definition and see how we should think of these groups.

First, a local church is made up of true believers. The intent should be that every member is a true Christian. But, as Jesus said, there may be tares among the wheat.

Second, a local church is comprised of *baptized* believers. It was the New Testament practice to add new members to a local church following their baptism. "Then those who gladly received his word were baptized; and that day about three thousand souls were added to them" (Acts 2:41).

Third, they must be in vital union with Christ and each other. A true church is not merely a group of people who carry out good deeds, perform religious ceremonies, and keep traditions. They are people who have been united with Christ *spiritually*. They know Him and He knows them. They live in spiritual union with Him through His Word and prayer, and with one another as members of the same spiritual family—parts of the same spiritual body, indwelt by the same Spirit.

Fourth, they must affirm and proclaim Christ's gospel. If a group of professing Christians believes and preaches a "gospel" that Jesus, or Paul, or any of the other apostles would have condemned as heresy, they may not be considered a true local church. Consider Paul's strong words in Galatians 1:8-9:

> But even if we, or an angel from heaven, preach any other gospel to you than what we have preached to you, let him be accursed. As we have said before, so now I say again, if anyone preaches any other gospel to you than what you have received, let him be accursed.

Paul was referring specifically to a distortion of the doctrine of justification by faith alone. But other heresies are also addressed in the New Testament. These would include any teaching that distorts or denies:

- the triune nature of the only God (Mormons deny this),

- the full deity of Christ (Jehovah's Witnesses deny this),
- the final authority and sufficiency of Scripture (Roman Catholics deny this),
- the inerrancy of Scripture (Many liberal churches deny this), or
- the biblical meaning of "justification by faith alone" (Roman Catholics deny this, as do churches who teach that water baptism, or any other "work" either saves or contributes to salvation).

Groups of professing Christians who hold to any of the above distortions or denials of Christian doctrine may not be considered true churches.

Fifth, a true church must submit to the headship of Christ in doctrine and practice according to His written Word. No church is perfect in this regard, but every true local church is constituted for this purpose.

What about differing views of baptism? Can a Christian group be a church if it does not practice immersion after conversion?

This question uncovers a difficult issue. As I discuss this, remember that I am not using "church" in the strictly English way of understanding the word, or even the broadest meaning of *ecclesia*, which includes civic assemblies. I am *only* referring to local churches in the biblical sense—groups of true Christians organized according to the commands and precedent of the New Testament.

Almost every group of Christians agrees that a person must be baptized before he may be considered part of a local church. Even paedobaptist groups require sprinkling or pouring (which they term "baptism") before admitting a person into membership. But as you know, they do this to babies—people who are not converted. Though I have many friends among them and hold many in high regard, I must assert again that such a practice cannot be considered baptism. The best that could possibly be said of such groups, when they are comprised of true believers, is that they are churches with a *serious* error regarding baptism. On the other hand, many would say that while these are groups of true believers, they are not true churches in the sense meant here. Remember the baseball team illustration.

What would you say about such groups? Do you consider them true churches?

Well, I believe a person must be baptized before being considered a member of a local church. Therefore, I define a local church as a group of baptized believers. I also believe those who were only sprinkled as babies have not been baptized. Now consider this scenario:

If I were to ask a Bible-believing paedobaptist pastor if he would receive an unbaptized person into his group's membership, he would undoubtedly say "No." Though he and I have differing convictions about what constitutes true baptism, we both agree that a local church is made up of baptized people. But what if I then asked: "If you were to come to believe that baptism is immersion *only*, and for believers *only*, would it be proper *then* for you to receive someone into membership who was sprinkled as an infant but never immersed as a believer?" If he were to answer "Yes" to the second question, he would be denying his own conviction as stated in his answer to the first question.

The point is, although people disagree about the definition of baptism, nearly everyone agrees that a local church is a group of baptized Christians—people who, in turn, baptize others. Where there are no baptized Christians and no practice of baptizing others, it is true that there may be an organized group of believers. And most people would consider such groups churches according to the common connotation of the English word or the broadest use of the Greek word. I would not contest such usage. But I would insist that where there are no baptized believers and no practice of baptizing new believers, there is no local church according to New Testament prescription and practice.

How should Christians handle disagreements about issues like baptism? For the sake of peace, should we simply lay our differences aside?

No, I would not say that. Where significant disagreements in doctrine or practice exist between true Christians, it is vital that we continue to love one another. At the same time, we must continue earnestly, gently, and patiently seeking to persuade our fellow Christians to see their errors. The fact is, the walls of disagreement between true Christians are grounded on firm convictions on both sides. But as I once heard a man say, we should keep the walls as low as possible and shake hands over them as often as possible.

Appendix 1:
Principles for Understanding Why Baptism Does Not Save

Some people believe that water baptism either saves or helps to save in some way, such as "completing" our salvation. They hold their views based largely upon a few verses, some of which can be quite confusing. Although grammatical and exegetical explanations could be offered for each of these passages, it is not my intent to be so detailed in this introductory work. Rather, let me offer some general help on how to approach such passages when we encounter them:

First, "belief" alone as the instrumental means of salvation is stated repeatedly.

Salvation is by grace *alone*, through faith *alone*, not by any works we could do (Romans 4:4-8; Ephesians 2:8-9). There are approximately 500 references to faith in the New Testament, many of which clearly state that it is the only requirement for salvation. Every time the doctrine of salvation through faith *alone* is emphasized, the doctrine of baptism as even a partial means of salvation is refuted by implication. The two doctrines are contradictory and simply cannot exist together. Whole books of the Bible were written to make it clear that no works are needed for our salvation other than the work of Christ. In many specific cases, the writers went out of their way to make this plain. Therefore, the few passages that seem to disagree must be interpreted by the consistent testimony of the many that are in agreement. Also, plain verses must be permitted to explain confusing ones.

Second, remember that all the groups that believe baptism saves or is necessary as part of salvation also believe in some way that justification is not finally secured until the end of life.

My view is different. I believe that good works are not saving, though they necessarily follow justification. They are the inevitable *result* of genuine conversion, but may never be thought of as the instrumental *means* of salvation. To these groups, faith *plus works* results ultimately in justification. The best they can mean is that they *are being* justified. I believe Christians *have been* justified (cf. Romans 5:1-2, etc.).

Third, the symbol fittingly represents the thing symbolized.

Baptism was closely linked to conversion in the early church. For the writers of the New Testament, it was unthinkable that a person would be converted yet not baptized. With this mindset, it would be easy for the writers to pass back and forth between the thing symbolized (salvation) and the symbol itself (baptism). This is why baptism and conversion are sometimes mentioned together as if they are one and the same event.

Water baptism so perfectly signified the experience of conversion that it sometimes appeared to actually be saving. That is confusing to us perhaps, but it would not have been to the early church because in the New Testament, symbols were commonly said *to be* the thing symbolized. As Baptist theologian J. L. Dagg notes,

In the language of Scripture, a thing is said to be that which it represents: thus, "The field is the world." "This is my body." "This cup is the new [covenant]." So Paul was said to wash away his sins in baptism, because it represented their being washed away. (*Manual of Church Order,* p. 17)

Fourth, an accoutrement to conversion may be used to convey the essence of conversion.

There are other accoutrements to salvation that are not saving in themselves, such as "confessing with the mouth." These are not saving acts, but accompany salvation. Therefore it is said, "whoever confesses Me before men, him I will also confess before My Father . . ." (Matthew 10:32). But confessing Christ before men is not the essential act necessary for conversion. Repentance and faith are the *only* necessities. By using terms like "confess" we *intend to convey* the essential things, but are using non-essential accompaniments of conversion to mean one must repent and believe in Christ. In the same way, the writers of the New Testament may have used "baptism," on occasion, to refer to "conversion."

Fifth, the mission of Paul was to preach the gospel, but not first of all to baptize.

The fact that Paul "was not sent to baptize" indicates that even though he thought baptism essential as the first act of Christian obedience, he did not consider it essential to conversion and therefore did not consider it his first task as an apostle (cf. 1 Corinthians 1:17). He even thanked God that he did not baptize most of the Corinthians (1:14), though they were baptized by others. Often Paul speaks about being a spiritual father to

49

people he did not baptize. Also, note that Jesus himself did not baptize, but rather his disciples. This is indeed interesting, if baptism saves and Jesus came to seek and to save the lost.

Sixth, the expectation that every believer will be baptized may cause the concept of baptism to be included when speaking about conversion.

The intention to obey all that God commands will be in the heart of every true believer. Therefore, if we say that a person must believe and be baptized, we are saying that he must believe with the full intent to obey, especially in this first act of obedience, water baptism.

Seventh, the nature of God's sovereign work in saving a person demands that baptism not be thought of as saving.

Salvation is of the Lord (Jonah 2:9; Matthew 1:21). God is the author of it, as He is the author of all things (Romans 11:36; Hebrews 12:1-2). We view regeneration (the new birth) as a sovereign act of God accomplished by His Spirit, not something accomplished because of any human action or decision (John 1:13; Romans 9:16; Ephesians 2:4-5; James 1:18). Even though repentance and faith are required of us (Luke 13:1-5; Acts 17:30), they are gifts from Him as they proceed only from hearts He has made alive (Ephesians 2:4-5, 8; 2 Timothy 2:26). But if we make baptism a requirement for salvation, we are saying that a physical human act plays a part in saving us. This is so contrary to the biblical position that it must be considered a denial of the gospel of God's grace. No Christian group having a biblical view of salvation, which is by faith *alone*, believes in baptismal regeneration.

Appendix 2:
Historical Quotes Concerning the Mode and Subjects of Baptism

The following quotes in various ways support the biblical view as to the subjects, method, or purpose of Christian baptism. However, many of these writers were right on one point while being wrong on another. I do not concur with everything that is quoted in the following pages. Read with discretion.

Early Church

St. Basil (Bishop of Caesarea from 370-379)
"How can we be placed in a condition of likeness to His death? By being buried with Him in baptism. How are we to go down with Him into the grave? By imitating the burial of Christ by baptism, for the bodies of the baptized are in a sense buried in water."

Cyril of Jerusalem (315-386)
"You are about to descend into the baptistry in order to be plunged in water. . . . For he who is plunged in water is surrounded on all sides by water" (*Catechism,* 3, 17).

St. Chrysostom (Greek theologian, 347-407)
"We, as in a sepulcher, immerse our heads in water. The old man is buried and sinking down, the whole body is concealed at once, then as we emerge the new man arises."

Pre-Reformation

Council of Celchyth (Canterbury, England, 816)

"Let ministers take notice when they administer the holy baptism, that they do not pour the holy water upon the heads of the infants, but that they be always immersed in the font; as the Son of God has in His own person given an example to every believer, when He was thrice immersed into the waters of the Jordan. In this manner it ought to be observed" (*Canon 6*).

Thomas Aquinas (Catholic theologian, 1225-1274)

"Baptism may be given not only by immersion, but also by affusion of water, or sprinkling with it. But it is the safer way to baptize by immersion, because that is the most common custom" (*Summa Theologiae,* Part 3, Quaest. 66, Art.7).

William Tyndale (Bible translator, 1494-1536)

"The washing [of baptism] preacheth unto us that we are cleansed with Christ's bloodshedding, which was an offering and a satisfaction for the sin of all that repent and believe, consenting and submitting themselves unto the will of God. The plunging into the water signifieth that we die, and are buried with Christ, as concerning the old life of sin which is Adam. And the pulling out again, signifieth that we rise again with Christ in a new life full of the Holy Ghost, which shall teach us and guide us and work the will of God in us, as thou seest Rom.VI" (*Obedience of a Christian Man,* 1571 edition, p. 143).

Reformation Era

Martin Luther (German Reformer, 1483-1546)

"On this account (as a symbol of death and resurrection), I could wish that such as are to be baptized should be completely immersed into the water, according to the meaning of the word, and to the significance of the ordinance, not because I think it necessary, but because it would be beautiful to have a full and perfect sign of so perfect a thing; as also, without doubt, it was instituted by Christ" (*Works,* 1551 edition, Vol. 2, 76).

"If you consider what baptism signifies, you will see that the same thing [immersion] is required. For this signifies, that the old man, and our sinful nature, which consists of flesh and blood, is all submerged by divine grace, as we shall more fully show. The mode of baptizing ought, therefore, to correspond to the signification of baptism, so as to set forth a sure and full sign of it" (*On the Sacrament of Baptism,* Quoted by Conant in *The Meaning & Use of Baptizein*).

"First, the name *baptism* is Greek; in Latin it can be rendered immersion, when we immerse any thing into water, that it may be all covered with water. And although that custom has now grown out of use with most persons (nor do they wholly submerge children, but only pour on a little water), yet they ought to be entirely immersed, and immediately drawn out. For this the etymology of the name seems to demand" (*On the Sacrament of Baptism*).

"Then also without doubt, in German tongues, the little word *tauf* [baptism] comes from the word *tief* [deep], because what one baptizes he sinks deep into the water" (*Works,* Vol. 21, 229).

"It cannot be proved by the sacred Scriptures that infant baptism was instituted by Christ, or begun by the first Christians after the Apostles" (*Vanity of Infant Baptism,* Part II., 8).

Ulrich Zwingli (Swiss Reformer, 1484-1531)

"'Into his death.' When ye were immersed into the water of baptism, ye were ingrafted into the death of Christ; that it, the immersion of your body into water was a sign, that ye ought to be ingrafted into Christ and his death, that as Christ died and was buried, ye also may be dead to the flesh and the old man, that is, to yourselves" (*Annotations on Romans* 6:3).

John Calvin (Reformer and theologian, 1509-1564)

". . . it is evident that the term *baptize* means to immerse, and that this was the form used by the primitive church" (*Institutes of the Christian Religion,* Book IV, Chapter XV, Paragraph 19).

Jerome Zanchius (Italian Reformer, professor at Heidelberg, 1516-1590)

"The proper signification of *baptize* is to *immerse*, plunge under, overwhelm in water" (*Works,* Vol. VI., 217).

Philip Melancthon (Scholar and Reformer, contemporary of Martin Luther)

"Baptism is *immersion* into water, with this admirable benediction [apparently referring to Matthew 28:19]" (*Melancthon Catechism,* Wittenburg, 1580).

Theodore Beza (Swiss Reformer, Calvin's successor in Geneva, 1519-1605)

"Christ commanded us to be baptized, by which word it is certain *immersion* is signified" (*Annotations on Mark 7:4*).

Post-Reformation

Joseph Mede (English scholar, 1600-1660)

"There was no such thing as *sprinkling* used in the apostles' days, nor for many ages after them" (*Discourse on Titus 3:5*).

Hugo Grotius (Dutch scholar, 1583-1645)
"That baptism used to be performed by *immersion*, and not by pouring, appears by the proper signification of the word, and by the places chosen for the administration of the rite" (*Annotations on Matthew 3:6; John 3:23*).

Jeremy Taylor (Irish bishop, 1661)
"The custom of the ancient churches was not sprinkling, but *immersion*, in pursuance of the meaning of the word in the commandments and the example of our blessed Savior" (*Commentary on Matthew 3:16*).

Bishop Bossuet (French Catholic bishop, orator and counselor of state, 1627-1704)
"To baptize, signifies to *plunge*, as is granted by all the world" (see *Stennett and Russen,* p. 174).

Joachim Neander (Lutheran theologian, 1650-1680)
"In respect to the form of baptism, it was in conformity to the original institution, and the original import of the symbol, performed by *immersion*, as a sign of entire baptism into the Holy Spirit, of being entirely penetrated with the same" (*Church History,* Vol. I., p. 310; *Planting and Training,* Vol. I., p. 222).

"Baptism was administered at first only to adults, as men were accustomed to conceive of baptism and faith as strictly connected. We have all reason for not deriving infant baptism from apostolic institution" (*Church History,* Vol. I., p. 311; *Planting and Training*, Vol. I., p. 222).

"We cannot prove that the Apostles ordained infant baptism; from those places where the baptism of a whole family is mentioned, we can draw no such conclusion" (*Planting and Training*, p. 162).

J. A. Turretin (Professor of Theology at Geneva)
"And indeed baptism was performed, in that age and in those countries, by immersion of the whole body into water" (*On Romans 6:3-4*. Quoted by Conant, *The Meaning and Use of Baptizein*).

Matthew Poole (English Puritan author, 1624-1769)
"It is apparent that both Christ and John baptized by dipping the whole body in the water, else they need not have sought places where had been a great plenty of water" (*Annotations on John 3:23*).

The Westminster Assembly (1644)
(From *Proceedings of the Assembly of Divines from Jan.1, 1643 to Dec. 31, 1644*, London, 1824, vol. 13, 300-301):

"One of the fascinating events in the story of immersion took place in England, where immersion was the common form of baptism until Cromwell's time. In 1644 the Westminster Divines met to discuss the matter. Dr. John Lightfoot, who presided at the Assembly, recorded the following.

" 'Wed. Aug. 7. This morning we met again. . . . Then fell we upon the work of the day; which was about baptizing of the child, whether to dip him or sprinkle, and this proposition, "Is it lawful and sufficient to sprinkle this child"—had been canvassed before our adjourning, and was ready now to vote: but I spake against it, as being very unfit to vote, that it is lawful to sprinkle when everyone grants it. Whereupon, it was fallen upon, sprinkling being granted, whether dipping should be tolerated with it. And here fell we upon a large and long discourse, whether dipping were essential or used in the first institution, or in the Jews' custom. . . . After a long dispute, it was at last put to the question, whether the Directory should run thus: The minister shall take water, and sprinkle or pour it with his hand upon the face or forehead of the child: and it was voted so indifferently, that we were glad to count names twice, for so many were unwilling to have dipping excluded, that the votes came to an equality within one; for the side was twenty-four—and the other, twenty-five: the twenty-four for the reserving of dipping, and the twenty-five against it; and there grew a great heat upon it.'

"The matter came up for discussion again the next day, but 'as for the dispute itself about dipping, it was thought fit and most safe to let it alone.'"

Presbyterians do not immerse babies because in the Westminster Assembly the decision was lost by one vote!

John Wesley (Methodist leader, 1703-1791)
"I believe (myself) it is a duty to observe, so far as I can . . . to baptize by immersion" (Moore, *Life of Wesley,* Vol. 1, p. 425).

"Mary Welsh, aged eleven days, was baptized according to the custom of the first church and the rule of the Church of England, by immersion" (*The Journal of the Rev. John Wesley,* Vol. 1, pp. 24). On May 5 he refused to baptize a child whose parents would not admit immersion (p. 29).

George Whitefield (Methodist leader, 1714-1770)
"It is certain that in the words of our text (Romans 6:4), there is an allusion to the manner of baptizing, which was by *immersion*" (*Eighteen Sermons,* p. 297).

Adam Clarke (Methodist commentator, 1760-1832)
"Alluding to the immersions practiced in the case of adults, wherein the person appeared to be buried under the water as Christ was buried in the heart of the earth" (*Commentary on Colossians 2:12*).

Moses Stuart (American biblical scholar, 1780-1852)
"*Baptizo* means to dip, plunge, or *immerse* into any liquid. All lexicographers and critics of any note are agreed in this" (Essay on Baptism, p. 51; *Biblical Repository,* 1833, p. 298).

Alexander Stourdza (Russian scholar and diplomat, 1791-1854)
"The church of the West has then departed from the example of Jesus Christ; she has obliterated the whole sublimity of the exterior sign. Baptism and immersion are *identical.* Baptism by *aspersion* [sprinkling] is as if one should say *immersion* by *aspersion,* or any other absurdity of the same nature" (*Considerations, Orthodox Church*, p. 87).

Modern

Professor L. Lange (German paedobaptist theologian)
"All attempts to make out infant baptism from the New Testament fail. It is totally opposed to the spirit of the apostolic age, and to the fundamental principles of the New Testament" (*Infant Baptism,* p. 101).

Edward T. Hiscox (Baptist leader, 1814-1901)
"Barnabas, the companion of St. Paul; Hermas, about A.D. 140; Tertullian, about A.D. 204; Hippolytus, about A.D. 225; Gregory, about A.D. 360; Basil, about A.D. 360; Ambrose, about A.D. 374; Cyril, about A.D. 374; Chrysostom, about A.D. 400; all speak of being

dipped, or *buried*, or *immersed*, or *plunged* in the water in baptism; and none of them make the least allusion to any application of water to the person for baptism, by sprinkling, pouring, washing, or any other mode whatever" (*The Standard Manual for Baptist Churches*, 1902, p. 95).

"The first authenticated instance of *sprinkling* occurred about the middle of the third century, or A.D. 250. This was the case of Novatian. The historian Eusebius gives this case, and Dr. Wall in his laborious reasearches could find no earlier instance; good evidence that no earlier existed. Novatian was dangerously sick, and believing himself about to die, was anxious to be baptized. The case seemed urgent, and as he was thought to be too feeble to be *immersed*, a substitute was resorted to, water was poured profusely over him as he lay in bed, so as to resemble as much as possible a submersion. The word used to describe this action (*perichutheis, perfusus*) has usually been rendered *besprinkle*; it rather means to pour profusely over and about one. This it was thought might answer the purpose in such an emergency" (*Standard Manual for Baptist Churches*, 105-106).

Philip Schaff (Noted Presbyterian church historian)
"Immersion, and not sprinkling, was unquestionably the original, normal form of baptism. Immersion shows the very meaning of the Greek word baptize" (*Schaff's History of the Apostolic Church,* p. 568).

John Wall (Episcopalian author)
"Immersion was in all probability the way in which our blessed Savior was baptized, and certainly the most used way of baptism" (*History of Infant Baptism,* Vol. 1, p. 571).

Dean Stanley (Anglican)

"For the first thirteen centuries the almost universal practice of baptism was that of immersion. They were plunged, or immersed in water" (*Christian Institute*, p. 17).

George Campbell (Scottish Presbyterian minister and President of Marischal College, Aberdeen)

"The word *baptizein*, both in sacred authors and in classical, signifies 'to dip,' 'to plunge,' 'to immerse,' and was rendered by Tertullian, the oldest of the Latin Fathers, *tingere*, the term used for dyeing cloth, which was by immersion" (*Translation of the Gospels*, Matthew 3:11).

Gotthard Fritzche (Lutheran theologian)

"But that, in accordance with the nature of the word *baptizesthai*, baptism was then performed not by sprinkling upon but by submerging, is proved especially by Romans 6:4" (*Commentary on the Gospel of Matthew*, Vol. 1, p. 120).

Wolfred Cote (Historian and author *The Archeology of Baptism*, London, 1876)

"In the primitive Church, and down to the fourteenth century, the ordinary mode of baptism was by immersion of the whole body in water. The original term baptize conveys the meaning of immersion, and no other. On this point we have most valuable testimony from the Fathers of the Church, and other ecclesiastical writers. They invariably designate baptism as the act of *dipping, bathing, or washing*" (*The Archaeology of Baptism*, p. 16).

Gerhard Kittle (Noted Greek scholar)

Kittle notes that during the time of Christ, "baptize" was used for "sinking of a ship or drowning" (*Theological Dictionary of the New Testament*).

Father B. L. Conway (Roman Catholic priest, author, and leader)

"Catholics are fully aware that the early practice of the church was to immerse, and that this practice prevailed in both the East and West in solemn administration of the sacrament to the end of the 13th century."

Henry G. Meecham (Greek scholar)

"Nowhere does the Bible show the sprinkling or pouring of water upon a person for baptism. There are seven New Testament passages containing the word 'pour', but none of them refer to baptism. 'Baptizo' is used 127 times and is never once translated 'sprinkling' or 'pouring.'"

Thayer's Lexicon

"to dip, immerge, submerge."

A.T. Robertson (One of the greatest Greek scholars ever)

Robertson went so far as to say that he questioned either the honesty or the scholarship of anyone who said that *baptize* meant anything other than "to dip, plunge, or immerse."

Christian Communicators Worldwide

CCW is a ministry based in Parkville, Missouri, a "river-stop" town in the Northland of the greater Kansas City area. We enjoy this quaint town with its beautiful park, interesting shops and eateries, and the stately Park University which overlooks it all. The meandering Missouri River, navigated by Lewis and Clark on their expedition, runs along the south end of the town. Independence, Missouri, the starting place for the Oregon and Santa Fe trails, is not far from Parkville. There is a lot of history here at "the beginning of the Westward advance."

Like those who explored and settled the western regions of the United States, CCW is also on a mission—to extend the message of Christ as far as God will allow. We do that through our websites (see next page) and through the speaking ministry of our founder, Jim Elliff. We also do this through Jim's writing ministry and that of his assistants, Daryl Wingerd and Susan Verstraete. CCW publishes books and booklets, offered by us and by other booksellers. Tens of thousands of pieces of free literature have also been distributed, both here and overseas.

Please visit our web sites:

www.CCWonline.org
This is our main site, with numerous articles, ministry tools, audio messages, and information about ordering our publications.

www.WaytoGod.org
This site contains articles and audio designed to guide interested people into a relationship with Jesus Christ. Here we also answer questions from inquirers.

www.BulletinInserts.org
This site provides timely and instructive bulletin inserts, handouts, and tracts. We offer free, downloadable inserts (also available in A4) for every Sunday of the year.